A Homemade Church

Bernard Palmer

VICTOR BOOKS

a division of SP Publications, Inc., Wheaton, Illinois
Offices also in Fullerton, California • Whitby, Ontario, Canada • London, England

Bible quotations are from the King James Version

Library of Congress Catalog Number: 77-89469
ISBN: 0-88207-658-2

VICTOR BOOKS
A division of SP Publications, Inc.
P.O. Box 1825 ● Wheaton, Ill. 60187

Contents

Author's Note

This book contains many personal stories of individuals and families. In some cases true names are used; in others it seemed advisable to change names and identifying facts. But the events are true as reported.

Preface

The ministries of Cedar Mill Bible Church in Portland, Oregon are broad and varied, but a golden cord of love runs through them all, drawing every participant together in Christ. A simple discipling program began in the early days of the church as Pastor Wollen ministered to individuals, and they in turn ministered to others. Steadily the leadership of the church expanded, reaching out in love to fellow believers and those outside of Christ. This church's uniqueness shines in its love and unity in the Holy Spirit.

1

Up From Failure

Like many cities across America, Portland, Oregon has split her seams and flowed around smaller neighbors with housing developments and shopping centers along ribbons of concrete that spiderweb the area. Nearby places like Milwaukie, Beaverton, and Hinsdale have been swallowed up, retaining their names and local governments but submerging their separate identities.

In 1946 the small congregation of the Cedar Mill Bible Church accepted a remote half-acre of pastureland for a building site, and some critics predicted the church would never amount to anything because the location was so far away from people. Today, though the road that leads from the freeway to the church dips and twists through shaded knolls and ravines, there is no shortage of people.

The large L-shaped, wooden structure with a brick tower at the front and a separate gymnasium building at the rear of a four-and-a-half-acre plot beckons invitingly to passersby. Christians moving into the area often seek out the church because of its reputation, and before long they are reaching out to the disinterested community members. Oregon has the lowest percentage of its population attending church of any state in the nation. If they are to get to church, someone has to go out and draw them in.

The congregation which had 80 members when Al Wollen assumed the pastorate a quarter of a century ago now numbers more than 1,000. Some families drive 25 miles to get to Cedar Mill Bible, drawn together on the Lord's Day from a network of home Bible study groups covering the sprawling community. These classes, under the direction of Pastor Al Wollen and his staff, form the hands and feet and mouths of the serving body of Christ at Cedar Mill Bible Church.

Pastors from up and down the coast have found their way to Cedar Mill to learn how to set up similar Bible classes among their own congregations. Others have invited Wollen to seminars in such places as Chicago, Toronto, Los Angeles, and cities in Central and South America to teach them his fruitful methods.

Sunday School leaders have pointed to Cedar Mill's education program as a model for others, and the preaching-teaching ministry is recognized as a key factor in the church's growth.

Doctrinally, the church is orthodox. Salvation by grace is preached, and there is a strong emphasis on evangelism in the home Bible studies. Significantly, Cedar Mill would rank with any church in the country in the percentage of church members who have become Christians as adults.

The attractiveness of the church is readily seen and understood by a visitor. "We believe very strongly that the church is a family," Pastor Wollen says. "And we try to look out for each other as loving members of a family."

On any Sunday morning during the fruit and vegetable season you can find long tables in the foyer filled with produce of every kind. Members with gardens and orchards bring their excess to the church and after the service people take what they would like to have. One member built a large dryer and set it up in the custodian's home next to the church so those who wanted to dry fruit and vegetables could do so.

The elderly in the congregation are looked after as tenderly as though they were everyone's grandparents. If someone has misfortune, the church deacons are there to help.

All of this is carried out in an atmosphere of keen concern for eternal souls.

"We constantly keep our primary purpose before us," Wollen says, "which is to build up Christians and to reach out to the lost. We strongly believe that we must express love and concern for each other if we are to do God's work."

To understand the Cedar Mill distinctives, it is helpful to know Pastor Wollen's background and the forces that shaped his life.

Twenty-year-old Al Wollen was grateful for the Sunday dinner at the home of the Bowes family in Montreal, Canada, but he was interested in little more than their well-laden table. The host had learned that Al was a convinced Jehovah's Witness, and so he didn't urge Al and his older brother Henry to go to church with them that afternoon. He explained that the family would be going to afternoon services at their chapel, and the visitors could wait for their return if they liked. Then Henry piped up that they would go along, and Al exploded inwardly: "You stupid nut!"

The whole misadventure had been Henry's doing. The

Wollen brothers had left their Saskatchewan home some weeks before to sell washing machines door to door in Montreal, a formidable task since neither knew more than a smattering of French. Henry had a certain amount of sales ability, enough to convince Al that his fortune, too, could be made in selling washing machines.

Sales were almost nonexistent, however, and their funds were nearly exhausted the morning that Henry knocked on the Bowes' door. In a moment he was inside, and Al, working the other side of the street, waited with growing excitement for him to emerge. The commission from a sale would mean they could have another good meal or two and hold out a couple of weeks longer. Al proceeded down the street and waited impatiently for Henry to show up, but he did not. Henry must be selling half the company, Al reflected.

Finally, when the entire morning had passed and it was past time to eat lunch, Al knocked on the door where Henry had disappeared. To Al's chagrin, he discovered that Henry wasn't selling anything—he had found the Bowes so congenial that he spent the entire morning visiting! Now both "salesmen" were invited to stay for lunch, which they were glad to do. Afterward they were asked back for dinner the following Sunday.

"I think I'm going," Henry said when they were walking away from the home of their new friends. "They're wonderful people."

Al decided he would go, too, but not because of the friendliness. "It was great to get a decent meal," he said. "A Sunday feed with those people ought to be something special."

But they didn't get to Bowes' the following Sunday. On Saturday night they got mixed up in a fracas, and about the time they were supposed to be putting in their appearance for Sunday dinner they were dodging the police in another part of town. Al took time to duck into a phone booth and apologize to the Bowes for not showing up for dinner. Mrs. Bowes graciously invited them for the following Sunday, and Al congratulated himself on his ingenuity in phoning. The brothers counted the days until they could sit down at the Bowes' Sunday dinner table.

Going to church was a high price to pay for any meal, Al fumed inwardly. But he promised himself he wouldn't listen even though he did go.

Still, he was curious when he learned that they were meeting in an empty store building. He had supposed a church had to have a gigantic edifice with stained-glass windows and cushioned pews and a pipe organ. The Bowes met in a store building that was as stark and unglamorous as a Saskatchewan barn, without beautiful pictures or statues or gothic ceilings.

The preaching Al heard that afternoon was very ordinary but somehow he found it intriguing. The pastor went through a brief passage of Scripture, explaining what the entire portion meant. His method was far different from that of the Jehovah's Witnesses ministers which Al was familiar with. These people would choose a theme and skip through the Bible to establish their point. Al assured himself that nothing he heard was either impressive or alarming.

The Wollen boys were invited to the Bowes' home the next Sunday and later they again found themselves in the "chapel." This time Al was furious. He was sure the pastor had planned his message with Al in mind. It was: "Hell and Who Is Going There." Anyone who knew anything about Jehovah's Witnesses was aware that they denied the existence of hell.

"I'll never set foot in this place again!" Al stormed inwardly. He wished he could voice his anger to his brother, but Henry wouldn't care because Christian teachings and the Jehovah's Witness dogma were equally unimportant to him.

The succeeding week was emotional torment to Al. There was no hell, he kept telling himself. Leaders Charles Russell and Judge Rutherford had made this a basic tenet of the Witnesses' faith, and Al believed it with all his heart. Or thought he did. He was so torn by doubt that he feared each step on the pavement might crack the cement and deposit him in the place he didn't believe existed.

As the end of the week approached, Al again faced a decision about going to the chapel. On the way to the Bowes house for dinner, he let his brother know how it was going to be that afternoon.

"If you decide to go to that meeting, it's OK with me," Al informed Henry. "But don't try to rope me into going. I've had it! I'll stay at the house."

His older brother shrugged indifferently. "They might not invite you back, but that's your business."

"I'll take that chance," Al retorted. And he would have carried out his plan if the Bowes' attractive daughter hadn't asked him to go with them. By this time Al was hoping she would like him well enough to go on a date, and a little cooperation seemed prudent. He swallowed his fierce determination to stay away from the chapel and tried to act as though he had been offered a second helping of blueberry pie. Digesting the invitation turned his stomach, however.

Again the pastor's message struck at the center of Al's being. "You must be born again," the pastor said, announcing the theme of his message.

It happened that a great controversy was then raging

within the Jehovah's Witnesses on that subject. Some leaders claimed the 144,000 reborn individuals destined for heaven had already been appointed. Other teachers claimed there was still space for those few who were different because of spiritual rebirth.

Al soon realized the pastor was talking about something entirely different than the Witnesses were disputing. This pastor explained Jesus' words in the third chapter of the Book of John, saying that everyone must be born again in order to see the kingdom of God. Spiritual rebirth occurred through faith in Jesus Christ, he said.

Confused and angry, Al was only dimly aware of the young man who approached him after the service and asked if he was born again.

"I don't buy that rubbish!" Al snapped.

The young man ignored Al's anger. "Would you like to talk to the pastor?" he continued.

"Yeah!" Al exploded. "I sure would!" He was going to tell the pastor what he thought of the drivel being dished out to these gullible people.

Al went into the pastor's study belligerent and determined. He came out meek and shining. The face-to-face discussion brought a clarity and conviction that led to Al's acceptance of Christ as personal Saviour and Lord.

Henry, who had been responsible for Al's going to the chapel, made a half-hearted profession of faith a little later, but it was years later when Al led his brother to a genuine relationship with Christ.

As Al walked home that night, he realized that Jesus Christ could forgive his sin only if He was God. As soon as he reached his room he got his Bible out of his suitcase and began to read. The farther he progressed during the next months, the more clear it became that Jesus is one with

God. This assurance opened an uncrossable chasm with the Jehovah's Witnesses.

But freeing himself from the deeply implanted teachings of Jehovah's Witnesses was a wrenching experience. Having lived with a Jehovah's Witness family as a child when his own mother was too ill to care for him, Al was thoroughly indoctrinated in the Witnesses' dramatic and momentous beliefs. The emotional struggle to escape all the entanglements did not end until he suffered a nervous breakdown.

Recuperating in Saskatchewan from his illness, Wollen spent endless hours studying the Bible with his family. Years later he looked back on this time as God's provision for his strengthening in true faith and his opportunity to reach his family for Christ. His parents and four sisters became Christians as a result of those Bible studies.

Al went on to Gordon College and Seminary in New England, and for a year after graduating he pastored a church in the area. Then, after hearing a message by Helen Baugh, founder and director of the Christian Business Women's Clubs, he was challenged by the need to reopen closed churches. Three young couples: the Paul Krohns, the Walter Stewarts, and Al and Roberta Wollen became the first workers for Village Missions. Mrs. Stewart and Mrs. Wollen are sisters. The Wollens pioneered that ministry on the West Coast for three and one-half years.

Early in Wollen's Christian life, he chose as his life's verse Galatians 2:20, "I am crucified with Christ: nevertheless I live; yet not I but Christ liveth in me: and the life which I now live in the flesh I live by the faith of the Son of God, who loved me, and gave Himself for me."

In theory he knew the meaning of the verse: as a Christian he was to exchange his own life for the indwelling life and power of Jesus Christ. Accordingly, the first eleven verses of Romans 6 were a frequent theme of Wollen's preaching, proclaiming how the believer died with Christ to sin and is alive to God through His resurrection: "in that he liveth, he liveth unto God" (v. 10).

In three and one-half years with Village Missions, Al was confident that God was working through him. Some 30 churches had been opened, with 13 missionary couples joining the staff to accomplish these goals. He had visited and analyzed the spiritual conditions of small-town churches throughout the four northwest states of the country. In doing so, he had pushed himself so mercilessly that his health gave out. A doctor told him that he had to change his work and find something less strenuous.

This was exceedingly difficult for him to accept. For months Wollen went through deep soul-searching. While immobilized by a blizzard for two weeks, Al found new spiritual direction. He realized he had misinterpreted God's will and work—that following God's plan in His way would not have led to exhaustion and bewilderment. In reality, Al wanted no program, no success apart from Jesus Christ. This was the "exchanged life" described by missionary J. Hudson Taylor and other Christians.

"Success" was no longer a quantity to be measured. Christ was not fashioning a program; He was making a man over into His likeness. Every day was to be lived in commitment to Christ, allowing Him to fill that day in whatever manner He saw fit. This did not exclude planning, but planning was not to overrule the redirections of the Holy Spirit in the details. Living was to be an adventure, accepting anything that God brought into it and recognizing that He was in control.

When Al came to Cedar Mill Bible Church, it was with a confidence that he could restfully take a day at a time, waiting to see what God was going to do in and through a new pastor and new people.

Waiting on God and moving as He led has demonstrated at Cedar Mill Bible Church that God makes no small plans.

2

Love Finds a Way

The roots of the village of Cedar Mill, Oregon sink deep into the nineteenth century. A lumberman by the name of Elim Young came to Willamette Valley in 1848 and established a saw mill on Cedar Creek among the large stands of timber that lined its banks and covered the nearby hills. Settlers were not long in following, and in 1852 they began to hold worship services in their homes. Thirteen years later the Wesley Chapel was built, and in 1891 its simple structure was replaced by a more imposing building of traditional, old-world design. Cedar Mill Bible Church was not born yet; its parents had not even arrived in the valley.

The new church was to come from a combination of Bible classes taught by the Rev. Forrest Forbes, a Miracle Book Club group, and a small Sunday School gathering. All together, the participants still numbered a bare 50. Forbes became the first pastor, then left after a few months to go to Chile as a missionary. Two other pastors came for brief periods before the Rev. Simon Forsberg settled in with a determined look late in 1943.

Forsberg was well known, having taught community-wide Bible classes for eight years in an abandoned church building. Under his direction the fledgling church took on new vigor.

In 1946 the Bonnie Slope Community Church united with the Cedar Mill group, forcing the expanded body to consider larger quarters. When a couple offered the congregation half an acre in the corner of their farm as a building lot, some scoffed: "Who wants to go to church in a pasture?"

But farmland had begun to produce urban dwellings, and with more faith than actual foresight the congregation accepted the pasture. When "urban sprawl" later enveloped Cedar Mill, the Bible Church was there waiting for the people.

Forsberg left in 1950 for a church in Montana, and the thriving congregation invited Al Wollen to assume leadership. As director of the Convention Department at Scripture Press Publications Wollen had been active in building Sunday Schools. He and his wife Roberta, whom he married in 1944 while in seminary, and their young son Bert moved to Cedar Mill after prayerful deliberation. The place and time proved to be right for a pastor with organizing and building experience.

But Wollen was more than a promoter: he was a shepherd of people. 'Way back on the Canadian prairies, Wollen had seen the value of small, closely knit groups. "There were warmth and a spirit of unity and fellowship that drew me close to the group," he recalls.

And in Montreal, where he received Christ as his Saviour, the 40 believers who met in the store front chapel were bonded together by adversity as well as love. In those days the Roman Church vigorously opposed Protestant evangelism. Windows were frequently broken by hooligans, and the evangelicals were jeered as they arrived for services. At times groups of youths would appear and throw stones at their meeting place.

Though the opposition was designed to discourage the little group, it had the opposite effect. The believers drew strength from one another and an intense personal relationship developed. There was no game-playing by anyone. A person either meant business with God or got out. The cost was too great for nominal Christianity.

"I saw how the people in that small group loved each other," Wollen says. "The persecution had much to do with it, but so did the fact that their numbers were small and they honestly cared about each other."

As a Village Missions worker, Wollen saw the force that could be unleashed when a small group of men and women started pulling together with singleness of purpose. Going into a community to open a church that had been closed for a generation or two sounded impossible, yet it could be done. He had seen others do it, and with God's help he did it also. A group of two or three believers working together, praying together, and sharing their joys and sorrows could get apparently hopeless situations moving.

"As far as I am concerned," he says, "this is and always has been a vital part of Christianity. It ought to be an integral part of every church, but all too often the intense personal relationships begin to disappear as a congregation grows larger."

Wollen was determined to develop and maintain this warm family relationship at Cedar Mill, regardless of how large the congregation might grow. At the time he didn't know how he would accomplish the feat. He only knew that it had to be done.

Like so many small churches, entire age-groups were missing at Cedar Mill Bible. The Sunday School had emphasized bringing children in, so it was made up of juniors, intermediates, and a few teenagers. The congregation still had, as its nucleus, the adult Bible class and the Miracle Book Club, an organization that promoted the reading of Christian books and the Bible. Both groups were made up of couples who were middle aged or beyond.

"We had hardly any young men or young married couples at the outset," Wollen explains. "The area was still rural with the nearest housing development two miles away. In order to reach the people we had to get buses and bring them in."

When Wollen accepted the call to Cedar Mill Bible Church, he asked the congregation to adopt the Quaker method of conducting church business. The church was never intended to have a democratic form of government, he told them; it was to be a theocracy.

"We became convinced that our responsibility was to learn the mind of God in any given matter and do it," he says. "We didn't want to have any personal projects to promote or axes to grind. If we did, the likelihood would have been that God wouldn't let us have our own way, anyhow."

The number of council members has increased over the years, but the church is basically governed the same as it was in the beginning of Wollen's ministry. The church council is made up of the two ordained ministers, six trustees, six deacons, and six elders. One third of the council members leave their positions each year, and are eligible for reelection after one year. A nominating committee appointed by the council chairman compiles a list of qualified people for council vacancies, from which the council selects a candidate for each vacancy. These people are presented to the congregation for approval, at which time other names can be submitted and voted on. The congregation also votes on the yearly budget and any changes proposed for the by-laws. All other matters are left to the council.

The council does not vote on its business in the normal way of counting "ayes" and "nays." When there is a point of opposition, the ususual method of conducting church affairs becomes apparent.

"We thoroughly explore the basis for opposition," Wollen explains. "We are particularly concerned about learning if there are any biblical grounds for the difference of opinion, or if there are any implications we are not aware of. We are very careful about taking action that would disturb the unity of our congregation or cause distress to anyone. No matter how urgent the business is, if someone on the council is opposed to it, we table the matter until we have had time to pray over it."

With but a single exception in the 25 years, the system has operated smoothly. In that case, one member objected to the way the church was governed and was fiercely determined to revert to the more common congregational system. He maintained it was not scriptural to have the council run the church.

"We have tried to let the Holy Spirit have full control in our church as well as our personal lives," says Wollen, "so it was imperative that we listen to our brother and try to resolve the matter in a way that would meet his objections and still follow what the council believed was the mind of God in their method of government."

Wollen explained the spiritual basis for the type of government they used, the way God had guided and blessed them in the past, and the assurance the entire congregation seemed to have that their type of government was God-ordained. But the dissident remained adamant.

The elders then met with the man twice, once spending an entire night in prayer with him. He would not budge from his conviction.

The problem came to an impasse just before the annual congregational meeting. Anxious to resolve the matter, the council gave the man the opportunity to share his position with the congregation and conduct a vote on the issue. If the vote went against the dissenter and he refused to accept it, the elders decided he would be dismissed from the church.

After the presentation, Pastor Wollen asked the people to vote on changing the bylaws for church government. Every single vote opposed the change.

Everyone thought the tremendous vote of confidence would settle the matter, but two weeks afterward the maverick phoned the pastor and suggested: "I've been thinking a lot about that vote; I believe we went about it in the wrong way." Reluctantly, the council asked him to leave the church. Almost 13 years later, the man called Wollen to apologize. "I've got to get something straightened out. I can't go on living in this bitterness. Will you forgive me for what I did to the Cedar Mill Bible Church and what I did to you as pastor?"

That call confirmed to Wollen that God led them in establishing their form of church government.

The congregation was still quite small when the need of a new building became apparent in the late '50s. The project was formidable, but an elderly crippled woman ignited the congregation's faith. She was living in near-poverty, and the deacons had done what they could to make her life more comfortable. As she hobbled out of the church one Sunday morning, she handed Wollen an envelope. "The Lord told me to give you this for our new church," she said.

To Wollen's amazement, the money order was for $100. That afternoon he went to thank her for the gift. "How can you possibly give this much?" he asked.

"I have quite a large family," she said, smiling. "For years my kids have sent me small checks and gifts of cash at Christmas and for my birthday. I've been putting that money aside, figuring that when the fund was large enough I was going to invite all my children to a party at a fancy restaurant. But when I was talking to the Lord the other day, He told me that my kids didn't need a dinner party—we need a church."

The gift stirred the congregation to similar faith and sacrifice. As they moved into a building program, God supplied an architect who had become interested in the church and had been led to Christ by Wollen.

A well-equipped neighbor dug the basement and furnished several hundred yards of crushed rock to provide a base for the parking lot, at just the cost of fuel for his bulldozer and trucks. A lumber mill sent 79,000 board-feet of lumber without charge!

With the outside basement walls in, a Saturday was scheduled for beginning the framing of the interior. Five carpenters and eleven helpers from the congregation offered their services, with only one, a superviser, on the payroll. Church women were coming at noon to prepare dinner for the crew.

An hour before starting time, cars began rolling into the parking lot. Wollen dressed hurriedly and went out to see what was going on. As nearly as the pastor could determine all the men were strangers.

"We're the framing crew for the Lloyd Center Development downtown," a spokesman said. "We heard this church is doing some building. We're not working today so we decided to come over and give you a hand."

In a single ten-hour day, the experienced crew and cooperating church members framed the entire basement area and the deck for the main floor. Not one of the outside crew, as far as anyone knew, was a Christian. The foreman, however, started attending services at Cedar Mill and was regular in attendance until the Lloyd Center project in Portland was finished. He came to know Christ through the church and went to his next job as a happy Christian.

The building progressed until one job remained. The plans called for a brick tower, but funds were almost gone and only the pastor and one other member of the congregation had ever laid bricks. Still, the council was so sure they had the mind of the Lord that they ordered the brick with the understanding they had 90 days to pay for it, and that God would somehow provide the laborers for the task.

The two "bricklayers" had been working only an hour when a man in his 60s approached. His granddaughter had attended the church when she was a little girl, he said, and had always liked it. He wondered if he might help. Soon he was slapping down three or four bricks for every one the other two put into the wall. He worked all day and said he would like to stay for another but he had an obligation in Tacoma that he had to fill or it would cost him $150. Happily the workers arranged for the church to pay the $150 and the stranger to continue laying bricks. On Sunday morning the congregation gave enough to cover both the bricklayer's cost and the bricks.

When the building project was launched, some members were concerned that contributions would be diverted from missions support. The missionary budget that year was $10,000—and when the building was completed in 1962 missionary giving had doubled to $20,000!

"We learned a valuable lesson during that period," Wollen says. "When a congregation has the mind of God on a matter, He will see it through and bless in all levels of the work."

3

Those Gifted Laymen

Wollen's preaching experience was strongly slanted toward reaching unbelievers with the Gospel. Sunday morning and evening sermons both included a direct appeal for non-Christians to trust Christ. As the Cedar Mill ministry progressed, Wollen came to see that he was misdirecting his efforts. As shepherd of the local flock, he needed to feed his sheep spiritually so the whole congregation could bring new sheep into the fold.

"For us," Wollen says, "this has been a turning point and the heart of any success the church has had." Evangelism is still at the heart of the church's ministry. One of Latin America's foremost evangelists, Luis Palau, is a member of Cedar Mill's congregation, but the emphasis has shifted from a pastor-centered evangelistic effort to a lay-centered outreach.

In Wollen's second year at Cedar Mill Bible, he visited the victim of a car accident and found her still unconscious. Wollen had contacted the Polettes in their home some

months earlier and had not seen them since. Now her re-
covery was in doubt and her husband was deeply concerned.

Every other day Wollen stopped at the hospital to see
how Mrs. Polette was doing—and found no change in her
condition. On the fourth or fifth visit he felt led to step
behind the curtain that shielded her from the others in the
ward and take her hand in his. Then he said, quite loudly,
"Mrs. Polette, you are going to live." He was acting on the
knowledge that the unconscious state does not always mean
the patient is completely out of touch with surroundings.
"Mrs. Polette, you are going to live," he repeated three
times. Then he spoke a short prayer and left.

The next time he saw Mrs. Polette, she had regained
consciousness and been moved to another hospital. Wollen
introduced himself and told her he had been praying for
her.

"I know," she said, smiling. "You told me I was going to
live."

Soon Mrs. Polette was dismissed from the hospital, and
the pastor began visiting her home. On one such visit Mrs.
Polette committed her heart to the Lord. As two church
couples lived near the Polettes, Wollen suggested they might
want to visit and encourage the new Christian. He also
indicated he would be willing to hold a Bible study in the
Polette home if the three families were interested.

The group was launched and grew rapidly as the participants invited their friends. Both the attendance and the
spiritual growth were impressive.

When Wollen had to go out of the city for a week, he
intended to suspend the class for that meeting, assuming
that he was the only qualified leader. But the loss of a
teaching opportunity seemed worse than a mediocre meet-

ing, so he asked Ernie, a barber who was Sunday School superintendent and a member of the home class, to take his place.

Ernie had no formal Bible training but he had been active in the Sunday school for many years and he liked people. But Ernie was dubious: he said he didn't know the Bible well enough to teach the way the pastor did. "That doesn't matter," Wollen reassured him. "Use your imagination and allow the Spirit to lead you." Reluctantly Ernie consented.

The class had an enjoyable time, and a few weeks later Wollen asked Ernie to take the class again while he was on vacation. By the time the minister returned the group had grown to 16. Feeling that everyone would benefit by being in a smaller group, the class was divided: Ernie and Wollen each took half.

Strangely, the lay-led class continued to grow while the pastor's class sputtered along erratically. It was not easy for Wollen to accept the fact that a layman could lead a Bible study that could be meaningful to everyone involved.

"Frankly," he confesses, "my first reaction was that it was a case of the blind leading the blind. I was concerned that more confusion than light would come from such meetings."

But Ernie's group continued to increase until it was so large it had to be divided again. Another member took over half of the class as discussion leader. Like Ernie, Ted was not convinced he could lead a Bible study successfully, but he was sure of his own relationship with God and he didn't need the position to build his own ego.

"The success of those two lay leaders underscored something that was making itself increasingly evident to me,"

Wollen says. "I was convinced that the gifts of the Spirit will appear in the body of the church when that body launches out willingly to minister to one another. At that point Christians discover what their gifts are and can develop them in ministries."

At first Wollen could not perceive how the inexperienced lay leaders could lead their groups to a closer walk with Christ. He tried to help them take a more ministerial approach to their teaching, adopting his methods for planning and delivering lectures. To his disappointment, neither of the men was interested in following his plan.

Neither was teaching in the accepted manner: natural discussion leaders, they devoted their efforts to keeping the dialogue on track and getting everyone to take part.

"Finally I realized that instead of trying to teach Ernie and Ted how to handle their classes, I should be trying to learn from them," recalls the pastor. He saw that the strength of their teaching lay in their two-way dialogue rather than in a monologue. They were meeting people where they lived and helping them to understand their own needs and to answer their questions.

"I learned a valuable lesson on the importance of listening," Wollen continues, "when I got to talking with a young convert about that time whose Christian life was weak and filled with problems."

The convert startled Wollen with his frankness. "If you want the whole truth, Pastor, you were bugging me so much from the pulpit about accepting the Lord, and nailing me every time we met to make a decision that I finally gave in to get you off my back."

The comment reminded Wollen of a message he'd heard from a missionary. "He warned about pressuring for a decision before the individual fully understands what it means to confess his sin and receive Christ, or is undecided about his willingness to pay the price of a committed Christian life. I resolved right then to stop talking so much and to spend more time listening."

The pastor was upgrading his education. "It fit in with what Ernie and Ted and their Bible classes were teaching me: if people are given an opportunity to express themselves, they not only learn quicker and better, they have chances to talk about their own concerns and hang-ups, and that enables others to know how to help others to know how to help them."

A Bible class member confirmed the insight from his own experience. "I had some real hang-ups before I was converted," he said. "I didn't realize until after I had received Christ how those things stood between me and salvation. It just happened that the preacher never mentioned or explained my particular hang-ups, at least when I was in church. But in Bible class we were discussing a passage that gave me a chance to ask about the statements in the Bible that really bothered me . . . I guess that's why I'm a believer today."

Other Bible class leaders have also learned the value of dialogue. They have seen the help they can be to an unbeliever or a new convert just by listening. Ellene Boden goes one step further. She announces to the members of her morning Bible class for women just before they break into smaller groups for the lesson that she will be in the kitchen to talk with anyone who has a heart problem.

"The first time I did that," she relates, "four women came in to talk with me. And they didn't do it because they thought I was an expert on counseling. Mostly I think they just wanted a concerned Christian woman who would talk with them about their problems and pray with them."

Rhonda was one of those who came to Mrs. Boden. She was desperately afraid that her husband was going to leave her, and Ellene guessed that her fear-born tension and bitterness was going to drive her husband away unless she changed dramatically.

Rhonda poured out her story, and Ellene said nothing until her overwrought guest had spent herself. When Rhonda, drained of her anger, fell silent, Ellene quietly helped her to examine her own attitudes and actions. Then they committed the need to the Lord.

"I took her hand," Ellene recalls, "and said, 'Now, we're going to give this to Jesus. We're going to hand this problem to Him and ask Him to solve it for you. By faith we're going to thank Him for the peace He is going to give you. We're going to receive the joy of His love!' "

Rhonda spent several minutes thanking Christ for taking her twisted life (she was a Christian but was not walking in the Spirit) and for giving her the peace and assurance that He would straighten out her personal problems and restore her marriage to what it ought to be. She left the Bible class serene, and the Lord began His work in her marriage.

"Quite a few of our gals have real problems with their husbands after they receive Christ," Ellene Boden went on. "It's so hard to make them see that they need to stop trying to change the men they have married and commit them completely to Christ."

Becky was married to an alcoholic who was everything a woman would not want in a husband. When there was no money for groceries, she would rail at him for spending his wages on liquor. She was constantly trying to get him to stop drinking and lying and making life miserable for herself and her family.

"It seemed that every time the Spirit of God would start to work," Ellene said, "Becky would get in the way, hindering Him. Through the help and encouragement and prayers at Bible class, she was finally able to stand aside and let God have His way with her husband. Today he is a believer, walking closely with Him. From the moment he trusted Christ he stopped drinking and their home has become what they both longed to have it be."

One young woman who worked in a factory and used profanity worse than any stevedore on the docks accepted Christ in Roberta Wollen's Bible class. Her husband, who was also an alcoholic, saw such a dramatic change in his wife that he went to see Pastor Wollen and gave his heart to Christ.

A 62-year-old woman who came from an entirely different church background started attending another study. "I learned more in one hour here than I have in all of my 40 years of married life," she told the group. "Last week when I got home I told my husband—for the first time since we were married—that I loved him. He reminded me this morning: 'Honey, don't forget to go to that woman's Bible study.' "

John and Debbie were members of the Bible class that met in Curt and Vi Neiss' home until John was transferred to Southern California. Debbie had been an opera star in Germany and John a successful Australian businessman. They met in a cocktail lounge in his country when she was there on tour.

After they were married and had moved to America, someone got Debbie interested in a Bible study in the city where they lived, and Debbie became a Christian. John wasn't disturbed by this new faith as long as she didn't try to pressure him into adopting it. "That's all right, dear," he would tease, patting her on the shoulder as she studied the Bible. "You go right ahead and read your little bookie."

They drove by Cedar Mill Bible Church often but paid little attention to it until the day they saw a sign announcing that Major Ian Thomas of England was speaking there. They didn't know who Ian Thomas was, but decided to go and hear him. After the service they surprised themselves by asking him to lunch the following noon. Major Thomas, who usually declines such invitations, surprised himself by accepting. At lunch John began to ask questions, and two and one-half hours later he asked Christ into his heart. It wasn't long until the vivacious couple joined the Bible class meeting in the Neiss home.

District Judge Bill Beers was not converted through the Bible study classes, but he has led a small study group of professional men in downtown Portland because of his conversion at the church.

"My wife and I had gone to a couple of nice churches, but listening to the sermons there was like being scratched where I didn't itch. Finally my wife started going to Sunday School at the Cedar Mill Bible Church and induced me to go along. I was so impressed I went back—six weeks later. The periods between visits kept getting shorter until I was attending regularly.

"As the conviction grew that I needed to make a decision, I kept sliding down this rope of self until I came to the big knot at the end. It was as far as I could go. I got hold of the pastor and in his study I accepted Christ as my Saviour. After that I had some rough personal problems, that saw my wife and me divorced and remarried after four years."

Now Bible study with his professional acquaintances is a spiritual highlight of his week.

For the past six years there have been from 40 to 60

home Bible classes meeting as an outreach of Cedar Mill Bible Church. More than 500 people are meeting to study the Scriptures every week, and at least a third are not members of the Cedar Mill Bible Church.

Several years ago, Wollen asked his Sunday congregation how many had become Christians as adults through the ministry of the church. One in four held up his hand. "That meant the home Bible classes were doing the job we intended for them," asserts Wollen.

The pastor of a church a mile away was strongly opposed to small groups meeting outside the church building. He felt controls must be maintained within the church. Then his people were attracted to the home classes of Bible Church members, and the pastor told Wollen he'd decided to start his own. Wollen was glad to share all he knew.

"That's exactly what I want to see," says Wollen. "There are about 200 Bible studies in homes along the valley now; I'm looking forward to the day when there will be 1,000."

4

Planning
to Grow

"In my early years at Cedar Mill," relates Al Wollen, "I used to groan under the burden of developing the spiritual life of our people. No matter how much I gave out on Sunday morning or Wednesday night, personal growth seemed disappointingly slow. But after our members got deeply involved in home Bible classes, they grew rapidly. In some of our people it was possible to see the growth week by week."

The new pattern for individual and church growth seemed to be divinely designed, but Wollen learned that careful human implementation was needed to produce satisfying results.

"I became the shepherd of the flock in a very real sense. The people became so concerned about their friends and neighbors that they began to pray for them and get them involved in Bible study. They not only sowed the Gospel seed but reaped the harvest. The pulpit was no longer the principal source of evangelization; that responsibility was transferred to the people in the pews. Yet the laymen needed guidance."

As the number and fruitfulness of the Bible classes increased, Wollen opened training sessions for leaders. Soon pastors from other churches joined the trainees. At present, the sessions begin on Friday evening and continue all day Saturday. During the past five years, more than 500 pastors and their people have come to Cedar Mill to learn how to put a home Bible class department together for their churches.

In addition, Pastor Wollen has conducted sessions all along the West Coast and in several distant cities of the U.S. and Canada. "I suppose I have had the privilege of training at least 1,500 people in seminars away from Cedar Mill," Wollen says. "In fact, the ministry has grown to the point where the church has made it a specific operation of the church. We have a manual that is being revised now."

Though the classes are laymen-led, the pastor is the key individual in the success of the program, trainees hear. For he must have a vision of what such a program can do for his church and the community. And he must be willing to put in the time to select, train, and supervise the lay leaders.

Wollen warns his fellow ministers against calling for volunteer leaders. "There is a temptation to go that route," he says, "because it is easier to recruit volunteers than to search out those who have the ability to lead but may have to be convinced of it.

"And leaders must have certain qualifications: they must possess spiritual stability, be living exemplary lives, and have the respect of others in the congregation."

Other important qualities are a love for the Word of God and for people, a facility for relating to non-Christians, and enough understanding of the Bible and confidence in the Holy Spirit to encourage questions and honest responses from class members.

Once class leaders are recruited, the pastor's training sessions begin. Leaders need to be taught the basic philosophy of the home Bible classes, how to conduct an effective discussion, how to lead shy individuals into taking part, how to deal with divisive and controversial doctrines, and how to keep the discussion moving along on the subject.

"Pastors have been trained to lecture and to preach," Wollen says. "Consequently we often have the idea that this method is the only way of teaching the Bible. This is not true, and it is especially wrong for home Bible studies. Overcoming this misconception removes a big obstacle in leading a class."

The pastor must actively promote the formation of classes, according to Wollen. He uses pulpit opportunities to focus interest on the Bible studies and to tie them into the total ministry of the church.

Though most participants in the Bible classes speak readily of the unity and love they experience, this is not an automatic or sudden development. Wollen recommends that studies begin with members of the church family who build unity and closeness of spirit for a period of months before reaching out to non-Christians.

Group members need time to learn to reach the place where they care about each other enough to share their inner thoughts and needs. When sharing stirs support and harmony in the group, it is ready to communicate a glad faith to the uncommitted.

Wollen stresses the importance of the pastor's regular contact with class leaders. Unless he knows what's happening—and not happening—the classes do not strengthen the overall ministry of the church. Sometimes the pastor needs to counsel a leader or directly intervene. Wollen describes one such situation that was corrected before it became serious.

"At our regular monthly meeting with the home Bible study leaders I questioned them about what they were teaching. It came out that one of the group was beginning to stress doctrine that I felt was divisive. I asked her to remain behind when the others were gone and I talked with her about it. The next month I talked with some in the class and found that she was continuing on the course I had asked her to change. So I felt it necessary to relieve her of her class.

"She was a young lady who had grown up in our congregation. My contact with my leaders is so close that I learned about this new development within two or three weeks after it began, so there was little time for it to cause us problems.

"There is probably no graceful way to relieve a teacher of a class, but I tried to be as kind as possible. I told her I had no quarrel with what she believed, but as I had explained to her, she was teaching doctrine contrary to what I believed and preached. It could cause confusion in the minds of some, especially the new believers, and might make trouble for the church. I stressed the fact that I hoped she would understand and would continue to worship with us. We were prepared for her to leave but were glad that she continued to come to our church.

"This is a danger that any pastor with a home Bible class program must face up to and be prepared to deal with. But this possibility should not deter any church from adopting the program."

Wollen served as coordinator of class leaders until the proliferation of classes required extra help. In 1968 Jack and Ellene Boden were asked to take over the responsibility of coordinators.

"We first got involved when a guy from church started a Bible class in our home," Jack recalls. "We had become Christians the fall before and in the spring we were asked to host a class. After a couple of years the leader's job took him away from Portland and I was given his class. After a few years of teaching, we were entrusted with seeing that the program had trained leaders in every group, that there were homes to meet in, and that interest was kept as high as possible. We took care of all the details of supervision that are necessary to make a program go."

One of the best sources for leaders is in the classes. "Members observe the leader, and those with aptitude for leadership soon are making strong contributions," explains Jack Boden. "So, when a leader is going to be away, we urge him to select someone from his group to lead. This helps us to learn who can handle discussions and can also make individuals aware of abilities they may not have known they had."

When Jack first accompanied Pastor Wollen to training seminars, he spent most of his time describing the mechanics of setting up Bible classes and supervising them. Now that Wollen has written two books* on the subject, Jack refers trainees to the books and emphasizes the exciting things that have happened in his life through the Bible classes.

It is often difficult to attract unsaved couples to a Bible class, but the Bodens have found a way.

"I don't know whether they are afraid of our trying to pressure them or what," Jack says, "but Ellene tries to get a wife interested in coming to a morning Bible class for

---

*How To Conduct Home Bible Studies, by Albert J. Wollen, Victor Books
Miracles Happen In Group Bible Study, by Albert J. Wollen, Regal Books

women. Then, after she's been coming for a while I call her husband and say, 'Hey, these gals are getting together and having a great time. Why don't we get involved too?' It's easier for the men to come when we do it that way."

The morning class that meets in the Boden home is an example of what can happen when women get burdened for a particular neighborhood. Ellene said she had never thought seriously about reaching others for Christ until she heard a Campus Crusade worker speak about the great opportunity.

"I prayed, 'Jesus, I have never led a Bible class, but You just work through me.'

"I wrote up some invitations and with great fear I went to the doors of my neighbors and gave them out. I didn't know what to expect, but I was so concerned I did it anyway. God was changing my marriage as He had changed my heart, and I wanted others to have the same joy and peace I had. I knew some of them were having deep troubles.

"Nobody was rude or unkind to me, but that didn't mean they were going to come. Only two showed up. One of them became a Christian, and I learned she had a Christian mother-in-law who prayed for her every day for four years before I came to her doorstep. After she received Christ she came to my house and the two of us prayed every morning five days a week.

"There were nine ladies we were praying for. We were so concerned for them and so impatient we wanted them all to become believers overnight. Within six months they were all attending regularly and we had the privilege of seeing all nine come to a saving knowledge of Christ."

Then they invited seven Christian women to meet with them and asked the entire group to invite others. The morning Bible class was up and away.

There was an immediate problem of caring for the young children of some of the women. That was solved by hiring baby-sitters from the congregation who would supervise the care of the children and also teach a 'Happy Hour Club' for the preschoolers who were old enough for it. The opportunity to reach the children was too great to allow it to slip by.

Soon there were 30 attending the Boden morning class, then 40, and finally it grew to 70. There were seven groups meeting in seven rooms, with a leader for each. Ellene taught a lesson for 30 minutes to the entire group; then they divided into smaller groups, each studying a different subject.

When it became apparent that the group had to divide, several women of Dutch descent who stuck together went to another home for a separate class. That study grew into 40-plus regulars.

Ellene became concerned about another neighborhood that had no Bible class. It was a section of new homes, and Ellene knew only one resident there. That one agreed to host a group, and personal contacts were made. In a few months 41 were meeting regularly.

"There are four groups in that home now with four leaders," Ellene says, excitedly. "They get together for two hours every Thursday morning. There are more women saved in that study than in any other I am responsible for. Every week they have from five to seven new people visit and many of them continue until they are converted, then a change of jobs takes the family away."

The Bible class influence reaches into church activities, sometimes surprising guest speakers. At a family camp a special speaker was interrupted frequently with questions.

"Hey," someone would say, "I don't understand that. Would you please explain it a little more?"

"It must be a shock to those who have never experienced it," Ellene comments, "but at least they realize the people are listening. We're so used to expressing our opinions and asking questions that it doesn't seem unusual or rude to us."

Bob and Dianne Bowles started attending Cedar Mill in 1972 or 1973 and immediately got involved in home Bible classes. The effect on their lives was immediate, though they had been Christians for some time. Before long they had assumed a position of leadership and were having a Bible class of their own.

The following summer they went back to their hometown in the deep south on vacation and shared with their friends and relatives what the Bible classes had done for them. Some of the family suggested a class be started immediately, and by the time the Bowles left 15 people were meeting in the new group.

In the months that followed, the young couple guided the class by telephone from Oregon. A spiritual awakening occurred in the church where their family attended, and seven home Bible classes were organized. When Bob and Dianne went back the following summer, the classes were strong and growing and the working of the Holy Spirit within the church was evident.

According to Vi Neiss, it is the working of the Holy Spirit that makes the Cedar Mill Bible Church unique—or "significant" might be more accurate, since the Holy Spirit is widely active today.

In Vi's opinion: "The emphasis on small intimate groups where Christians can grow to care for each other has helped to create the sort of spiritual climate which permits the Holy Spirit to work."

Yet the center of church life is still where the congregation gathers for worship, instruction, and prayerful direction.

"The reason Cedar Mill is flourishing today is the strong preaching we hear from the pulpit every Sunday," said one young man.

A woman twice his age echoed the conviction. "Pastor Wollen challenges us to let the Holy Spirit have complete control of our lives. Our pastor teaches us what the Word of God says and shows us by his example how to live for Christ."

Wollen confirms the strong emphasis on the Spirit-filled life in his preaching. "Galatians 5:22-23 are the guiding verses of our congregation," he says. 'But the fruit of the Spirit is love, joy, peace, longsuffering, gentleness, goodness, faith, meekness, temperance: against such there is no law.' "

So pulpit lecturing and Bible exegesis have their place. And so do dialogue and sharing your brothers' burdens.

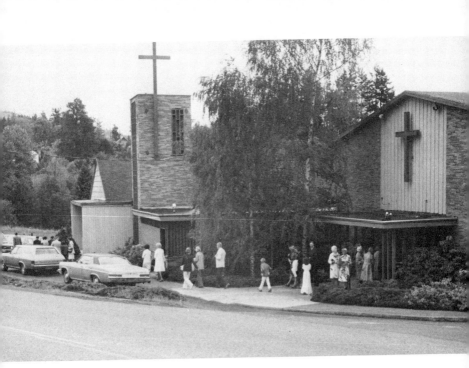

Sunday morning at Cedar Mill Bible Church

Walter Stewart
Assistant Pastor

Each Sunday morning
the church council prays
for written requests.

Pastor Al Wollen (left)

Hospital visitation

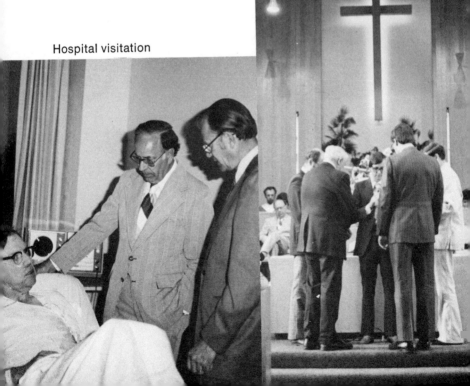

Church Council

Pastor Stewart with the Christian Education Board

One of two services on Sunday morning

Adult choir

Church office manager

Church librarians

Mrs. Joanne Cook
Director of tape ministry

First home Bible study

A young marrieds home Bible study group

A birthday celebration in the 2s and 3s department

A class in the high school department

Girls soccer team

Recreation in full-sized gym

Counseling in Pioneer Girls

Boys hockey team

5

Koinonia
Is the Greatest

Walter Stewart and his wife Laura came to Oregon immediately after graduation from Gordon College in Massachusetts to serve the Lord with Village Missions. Since Laura is Roberta Wollen's sister and both couples worked with Village Missions, they had more than a little in common. Yet they hadn't expected to serve together in the same church. That prospect developed in 1971.

Walter studied at Western Bible Seminary, then pastored three churches for almost 20 years. Illness in the family at that point led him to take a leave of absence from the pulpit. He went into commercial painting for a year and was looking for work when the thriving Cedar Mill Church was seeking part-time help in church visitation. Assistance was also needed in coordinating the Layman's Institute. Stewart accepted the assignment on a temporary basis.

The church council liked the results, and eventually they asked Wollen if Walter should be offered a full-time, permanent position. Wollen was skeptical at first, as Stewart was also when approached on the subject. The relationship of their families could produce complications, but after earnest prayer the move seemed to be the leading of the Lord. So Walter Stewart became assistant pastor, and Cedar Mill Bible picked up momentum.

Sunday School attendance was struggling at the 300-level when Stewart zeroed in on it. "The most important change we made was in the curriculum," he says. "We set up a program of elective classes for the adults that seemed to spark the entire Sunday School."

Motivated adults brought their children, and the slumping attendance began to climb toward a new average of 600.

Pastoral visitation was Stewart's major responsibility: new families to call on, absentees, the ill, and the shut-ins. Visitation and phone calls demonstrate the church's interest in their people. Rather than depending on official membership pledges for loyalty, Cedar Mill Bible stimulates participation by loving interest, and bypasses emphasis on "joining the church."

Leadership is drawn from the "active members," those who have professed faith in Christ, expressed agreement with the church doctrinal statement, and maintained regular attendance. Weekly records keep the pastors posted on absentees—for helping, not hounding.

"If folks miss a couple of Sundays in a row," Stewart says, "my wife Laura phones them—she doubles as my secretary. Often a family has gone to visit Grandma or is taking a brief holiday, but if there are problems in a home, or illness, we try to follow through. It's surprising how many are having difficulties and would like to talk to the pastor. They may be reluctant to make the first contact, but when we have expressed our concern they are not so hesitant to ask for a visit from Pastor Wollen or an appointment in his office."

Not everyone senses the positive aspects of the phone checks. One new couple was phoned three or four times over a period of several months and they complained to Wollen. "What's going on here, anyhow?" they asked. "Are you a police department checking up on everyone who's absent?"

"That isn't the idea at all," they were told. "We're interested in the folks who come, and if they stop coming we'd like to know if we can do anything to help."

"Well, we don't like it. We don't want to be checked up so closely. If we decide to miss a Sunday or two, we don't care to have everyone know about it."

"If you don't really want to be a part of the family here and aren't interested in being checked on," the pastor told them, "I would suggest that you go to another church. We feel we should keep in touch with all our people."

This family left, but returned a year later. At the service that Sunday morning, they told the pastor, "We've decided to come back to a church that really cares for us and ministers to our needs."

Stewart was also involved in organizing a new kind of fellowship group called Koinonia, the Greek word for communion or fellowship. It developed through a need felt by several young couples in the church.

Lynne Franz had grown up in a church Walter Stewart pastored, and she and her husband came to Portland to go to school. Nancy Anderson and her husband heard about Cedar Mill Bible Church from friends, and came looking for a Bible study group they could join.

"Nancy and I met the first Sunday we came to church and became friends right away," Lynne recalls. "We loved the church, but we were disappointed that there was not a flourishing 'young married' group."

Lynne and Nancy became prayer partners, and in the fall the Andersons started a home Bible class for young married couples.

The initial four couples increased rapidly as the church office referred new couples to them. It wasn't long until the group had to be divided, although they still met in one home.

"A number of unbelievers came," Nancy recounts, "but we regretted that we didn't have enough opportunity to know them better. We met for Bible study, then went home, feeling that we should be spending more time together."

The following spring Walter Stewart suggested a planning meeting to see if they could work out some activities that would build friendships and reach out to new people. Eight or ten couples came to the meeting, and the Andersons, the O'Neils, and the Franzes were elected to a planning committee.

This marked the beginning of the Koinonia groups (not connected with the national organization of that name). Koinonia differed from the home Bible classes in featuring additional social activities such as basketball, volleyball, and varied outings. Their goals were the same as those of the Bible classes: to provide spiritual fellowship for believers and promote evangelism among nonbelievers.

Their first schedule of activities for the summer included camping trips, hikes, a retreat, and volley ball. Later they decided to start a Sunday School class for their group. They went to the superintendent and told him what they would like to have, volunteering to teach it themselves. The men rotated teaching for awhile, then began praying for a regular teacher. Walter Stewart took over that responsibility.

The Sunday School class started with five couples and mushroomed to fill the room they had been given. They scheduled a variety of social activities: parties, progressive dinners, and co-host dinners in which two couples from the church entertained two couples who were newcomers.

Activities changed along with the group development. One of the members said, "When four couples get together now, the chances are that there will be eight or ten kids in the group as well. We discovered that what was practical when we were just married could be cumbersome when we have children."

The Koinonia group operated as the church's Young Married category until they were hit by a baby boom in late 1974. Stewart convinced the group they had qualified for graduation, and they became K2, while a new Young Married group was organized. There is also a K3 and a K4 group, with divisions made roughly according to age.

"The key to the success of Koinonia is organization," one member said. "Our planning committee creates our agenda for several months in advance. We usually have one social a month, plus our weekly home Bible class and our Sunday School class."

"Another key is prayer," added a planning member. "We pray as we plan and over everything we do. We encourage everyone in our group to have prayer partners to share their innermost concerns."

The Lord used the Koinonians in their special endeavors. Glen was taking graduate work when he and Debbie first attended Cedar Mill Bible. Pastor Stewart asked one of the Koinonia couples to go with him to visit them. Afterward the K couple made several more visits, and the newcomers started coming to the Sunday School class.

Glen didn't think he could take time for the home Bible

class or social events, but when he finished his thesis the whole Koinonia program drew them in. Not long afterward Glen trusted Christ as his personal Saviour, joining his wife, Debbie in faith.

Jim and Glenda were Christians when they started attending church and a home Bible class, but Glenda was so quiet about her faith most of her friends didn't know she was a Christian.

"I didn't see how she could be," one of them said. "When I first met her we were hardly on the same wave length."

Then God began to speak to her through His Word. She began to attend one of the women's Bible classes as well as our evening class. Then her husband went with her to some of the retreats where they prayed and read the Bible together. That was the turning point.

"You could see Glenda blossom. She loves the Lord so much that He has become her chief topic of conversation. Her influence and testimony brought two of her neighbors to know Christ."

In the spring of '74 the group learned how closely knit it was. Three of the men were graduating—Lloyd from law school, Ken from the school of nursing, and Glenn was writing his master's thesis.

"The hurdles for each of them were big and we were all so concerned we were praying for them 20 times a day," one of the group explained. "Lloyd was out of town when the fact that he had passed the state bar exams was published in the Portland paper. We were all so excited about it we had to phone him in Grant's Pass and give him the news."

When Ken was away taking the state tests, friends called his wife continually to learn how he was doing. There was great rejoicing when he passed.

"You never know what friends can mean to you until something like this comes up," his wife said gratefully.

Lloyd, a young attorney, was accepted by the FBI and took training in Washington D.C. before assignment to a new location. His wife had to assume the responsibility for selling their home, boat, and a car and supervise the packing of their household goods.

Everything worked out better than the husband expected, allowing a larger contribution than usual to the church missionary fund before they left.

The Koinonians presented a keepsake quilt made by the wives, each block bearing a promise from the Bible and the name of the one who sewed it.

"Actually," Walter Stewart added, "The entire church is one big family in Christ." "Yet the group seems to have a love for each other that is all their own. It is wonderful to see."

And, no doubt, wonderful to experience.

6

Fun, Sports, and Discipleship

Anyone who has worked in church youth programs knows the exhilaration and despair, the rewards and failures, that accompany youthful idealism and brash inexperience. The casualties are tragic and the victories are momentous, making the church youth ministry one of the most critical of all.

At Cedar Mill Bible, the emphasis is on discipleship, or spiritual training, for all who are willing to pay the price of the more abundant life offered by Christ. That doesn't mean there's no fun and social activities for Cedar Mill kids, but that the church recognizes entertainment and snappy programs alone will not mold youth into mature Christians.

Since early 1975, Wes Hurd has directed his ministry as youth pastor. His emphasis on discipleship stems from personal experiences and training.

Wes was a so-so Christian in high school, along with being an outstanding student and football player. The "so-so" part let him down after his team won the league championship and Wes went out "on the town" to celebrate with a buddy. The resulting misconduct caused Wes' suspension from team participation in the state tournament. It was a bitter blow that he never forgot.

Not long before he was to leave for college, the Holy Spirit convicted him of his wayward life and directed him toward Christian training in college and seminary.

At Southern Oregon University Wes met a Christian leader on campus who was also an All-American quarterback on the football team. "Through him I got straightened out spiritually and learned the importance of a training relationship with more mature Christians," Wes explains. "Here I have been working on one-to-one relationships in my position as youth pastor at Cedar Mill. Right now I have five sophomore guys in a discipling program—on a voluntary basis. In addition we have Bible studies with a small group of high schoolers who have discovered some of the excitement of feeding on God's Word and want to grow."

Hurd regards the junior high and early senior high years as the most critical in a kid's life. It seems the staff has to knock itself out to hold the kids it has and to reach out for those on the fringe. A diversified program, with camping, bicycle trips, and special events attracts interest in the summer with its extra free time.

Four parent-couples rotate in hosting the Sunday night program in their homes, and three college-age people work with the junior high group. They teach a midweek Bible study, divided into small groups. A combination of parents and college students are sponsors and counselors on getaway events. Wes' wife, Carol and four other young women help with the personal discipleship of the girls.

"It is interesting to notice how the type of activity

influences the number who turn out," the dark-haired youth pastor observed. "If we have a social we can expect as many as 60 or 70 to come. If we hold a Bible study on a typical Sunday night we will have from 25 to 35. But if we have a serious Bible study where we really get down to cases with the kids, we can only count on five or six guys and about the same number of girls."

In the last year four young people have gone into some kind of full-time ministry, such as Youth for Christ or Campus Crusade. Hurd anticipates that perhaps a third of the present 30 who are regular in attendance may choose one form or another of Christian ministry.

Though the staff at Cedar Mill Bible Church is comparatively small, they have found a full-time recreation director to be a vital member.

"Our gym and recreation program plays an important part in our outreach," Pastor Wollen says. "Interest in sports here is high, and there are a number of families who have received Christ because they started coming to church through our volleyball or basketball competition."

The commodious gymnasium was the vision and provision mainly of one man, not the church planners. A member was so convinced of a gym's value in attracting young people that he donated most of the funds for the building.

"The gym has been a most effective means of drawing people from the community," says Wollen. "It has also helped us in building the family relationship we covet for every person in our church."

Jim Wells, the director of recreation, was hired on a part-time basis more than three years ago; then the job developed into full-time.

"We still don't have our entire program operating," he

says. "It may take another three years to establish all the things we feel God would have us set up. We are moving forward, adding new activities as we are able."

They now have a year-round sports program, beginning with minibasketball in a league for third-, fourth-, fifth-, and sixth- grade teams, and the "Ben-Gay League" for men 26 years of age and over. There is also volleyball, hockey, and in the summer archery and other activities.

Currently there are 15 basketball teams with two coaches to a team and a total of 200 kids taking part. Plans are underway to organize a junior high league. Once it is operating smoothly, Wells wants to start a high school league, which would enlist athletes not playing on the school teams, and possibly a league for the college and career group.

Wells tries to use different coaches each year in order to involve as many adults as possible. "I used to be concerned about finding coaches who knew the sport well," he confesses, "but in the church where I last served I asked for volunteers to coach a girl's softball team. The only one who volunteered was a gray-haired grandmother and widow who didn't know anything about softball. The first thing she did was to get the girls together and pray with them. Then she appointed a girl as captain and informed them that they were going to win the championship. They not only accomplished that, but every girl on the team was a Christian before the season ended. Here's where I learned availability and a love for kids are far more important than expertise in the sport."

The grade schoolers are required to attend Sunday School at least half the time to be eligible for basketball competition. They also have to write out a summary of the Sunday School lesson to show they didn't park their minds in the foyer with their jackets." In addition the coaches are expected to have devotions and prayer time with their teams.

"We're still experimenting with various approaches to teaching spiritual truths and Christian living," Wells says frankly. "We are not satisfied with the methods and results so far."

One fifth-grader started coming to Sunday School solely to play basketball, but as a sixth-grader he professed faith in Christ. Then he brought eight other boys to join the program. A number of the group, including the recruiter stayed on to join the service club program for seventh-graders.

A third-grader from a separated home had never taken part in organized sports. The kids at school picked on him because he didn't have much athletic ability. The boy's mother was so fearful of the scorn of teammates that she hesitated allowing him to play.

"He did have trouble at first," Wells recounts. "Kids can be merciless, but the coach changed it all around. Tactfully, he convinced the players to praise the boy's efforts, and the idea caught on. When the season was over, he was voted the most improved player in the entire program."

This boy was responsible for getting his mother to attend Sunday School and church, breaking a 20-year habit of non-churchgoing.

Twin boys in one church family had the unusual experience of playing one entire season without winning a single game, then not losing once the following year. "It has been interesting to me," their mother said, "that the boys learned much more about teamwork and sportsmanship the year they lost all the time, than they did in winning. To me, that says something about the kind of coaches we have, who can turn a poor season into a victorious one. And it shows the emphasis of the entire program, which is not on winning, but on teaching Christian principles and character."

The Ben-Gay League also has an effective outreach. One young banker has brought three or four of his co-workers into the league. Another participant talked so enthusiastically about the fun that his boss began to make a 45-minute drive from his home to the church to play too.

"Our spiritual emphasis in the adult league is more casual than with the kids," Wells says, "but it is still an important part of every game night. We have prayer before each game and we always ask for prayer requests. We have had at least two families who have received Christ and joined the congregation because of this League."

The spiritual results are the rewards of all the effort and money expended. "We always try to remember that our goal isn't recreation—it's reaching people for Jesus Christ." The healthy bodies are a bonus.

7

Go Into All
the Neighborhoods

Having 500 children in Vacation Bible School classes would delight most churches, but that attainment didn't satisfy Cedar Mill Bible Church. "For a number of years we conducted Vacation Bible School in our church," director Mrs. Laurel Wantz says. "I suppose we were successful in a way, but we longed to see our summer program reach unchurched kids in the valley, and that was not happening."

And though the VBS attendance was impressive, Mrs. Wantz realized that many mothers found the necessary chauffering a burdensome chore. With these drawbacks in mind, the VBS director conceived a new approach (though the plan had been used successfully by other churches, she discovered later).

If the kids from unchurched homes would not come to church for Vacation Bible School, why not take the school to them with club meetings in the backyards of various neighborhoods? "I figured that mothers might be willing to let their kids go to a meeting on their block if they didn't have to be involved with transportation or paying out any money," she recalls.

The plan caught on quickly. Natural locations were areas where church members lived, especially regular VBS workers. Some women volunteered to provide the location if the church would supply the staff and material. Strategic and flexible like the home Bible classes, the Backyard Clubs reached into the neighborhoods daily for two weeks, some gathering in the morning, others in the afternoon and evening.

The typical meeting lasts for an hour and a half. It usually opens with a time of singing and a puppet show or other feature and a missionary story. A refreshment break is cookies and some kind of cold drink and a half hour class period, followed by a Bible lesson and a Scripture-memorizing time. Then it's "good-bye" until the following day.

Usually age four is the youngest a hostess will accept, though there are exceptions. Some three-year-olds are so anxious to come that the hostess or teacher will allow them to, providing they are cooperative.

On the final day parents are invited to a picnic and program. The kids sing songs and recite Bible verses or present some aspect of their daily activities. Instead of a picnic, some leaders take the kids on a special outing.

Attendance jumped to 700 the first year of the Backyard Clubs, and continued upward yearly to 1,000. There are now 17 clubs, a number of them being taught by high school guys and gals with junior high helpers. The teen-agers too are excited about reaching children for Christ.

"We older ones are also caught up in the excitement," says Laurel Wantz. "By taking the program out of the church to where people live, we have had Mormons, Hindus, and practically any religion you can name represented in our Backyard Clubs."

The purpose of the clubs is basically evangelistic, and the lessons are aimed at children who do not know Christ. The staff has adapted regular Vacation Bible School material to suit their out-of-doors conditions.

Church kids are usually the key to attendance in any club. "If we have two or three Christian kids in a neighborhood," Mrs. Wantz says, "we know we'll get a crowd. All they have to do is to talk about the fun they are going to have, and the unchurched kids will clamor to get in on it."

The plan of salvation is clearly presented, but an attempt is made to avoid pressuring the children into making a decision. "One of the workers explains: 'If a child likes his teacher, there is a temptation to do what he thinks she wants him to. He might indicate he has received Christ without really understanding what it means. So we present Christ and tell the kids the decision is theirs. Youngsters who make a commitment to Christ seem to tell the teachers voluntarily. The growth in faith comes through Pioneer Girls, boys club, or the subsequent weekly Bible clubs related to the church.' "

When a youngster makes a profession of faith, the teacher fills out a card. Another organization in the church reaches into that home in an effort to get the rest of the family involved in church activities. But the hostess plays the most important role in the follow-up.

"We have found," Mrs. Wantz says, "that the most effective means of following up on converts is to have a regular Bible club meeting each week in the home of the hostess (Cedar Mill Bible Church cooperates with Portland's Union Gospel Mission in the weekly Child For Christ Bible Clubs which the mission sponsors). The child usually knows her well as the mother of a good friend, and he feels comfortable going to her place.

"My long-range goal is to have such a club meeting all year in every home that sponsors a Backyard Club," says Mrs. Wantz. "If we could do that in addition to our summer program, we could be sure that the converts would be properly grounded in the Word of God."

Some of the teachers got involved in the program reluctantly. "I liked it when it was held in the church," one said, "but I'm not about to try to teach in somebody's backyard."

She had taught Sunday School for years with excellent results, so Mrs. Wantz urged her to reconsider—for just one week. Hesitantly she agreed.

"I can't believe it," she said after the week was up. "The children sit and listen to those stories in a way I've seldom seen—even in Sunday School. It's tremendous!"

The difference, according to Laurel Wantz, was that the majority of the kids in the Backyard Clubs didn't go to Sunday School and church, so they had never heard the Bible stories. And many of them had never experienced the attention shown by someone other than their parents.

Pastor Wollen is solidly behind the backyard program and is excited about its outreach. "We want to see every new believer involved in the activities of the church," he said. "And, of course, we would like to see all of those reached by our people become a part of our church family, but in many cases that is not practical. We encourage them to come here or to attend the evangelical church nearest them."

Without taking a scientific survey, it's safe to say that many new people choose to drive farther in order to become part of the Cedar Mill Bible family.

8

Blessing the Little Children

Johnny was upset at being left at church without his mother. Everything in the big room was strange to him. He didn't know any of the kids who were there or the big man who took him in his arms.

Johnny wailed plaintively—that would bring his mother back—but this time she kept going. Johnny was sure he would never see her again.

Then the kind man who was holding him said, "Have you ever seen a gerbil?"

Johnny shook his head. He didn't know what a gerbil was, but it sounded interesting.

"We've got some over here. Want to see them?"

Johnny stopped whimpering and nodded.

The pleasant man took him over to the cage where the little animals were playing. After a moment or two, while Johnny watched the gerbils with growing interest, the man opened the cage and took one out.

"You can hold him if you want to," he said.

That took a bit of thinking on Johnny's part. He wanted to hold the sleek, lovable-looking creature, but he wasn't sure if it would bite him. He looked up at his new friend for reassurance.

"He won't hurt you. See?" The man held the gerbil close and Johnny probed the gentle animal's soft fur. An instant later he was holding him delightedly in his chubby arms. About that time the boy's mother, who was listening around the corner, became aware of the fact that her son was no longer crying.

The following Sunday when she brought Johnny to his classroom, he went directly to the man who had been so nice to him. This time he didn't cry at all. He would soon be going from gerbils to the other learning centers where he would begin to hear about Jesus and His love and watchful care.

When Walter and Laura Stewart began to serve full-time at Cedar Mill Bible Church, Roberta Wollen asked her sister to help with the two- and three-year-olds in Sunday School. It had been a number of years since Laura's children were that age, and she had never specialized in students so young. But she and her husband had come to help wherever they could.

"I'll never forget the first Sunday morning when I walked into the Two and Threes," she says. "I had forgotten how tiny children of that age are—I felt like an elephant."

As she moved about, one of the teachers attracted her attention. She was kneeling on the floor so she could make eye contact with the children, and they were reacting to her in an amazing way.

"There I got my first lesson in handling two- and three-year-olds," says Laura.

According to Pastor Al Wollen, the department for

children of that age is the most important in the Sunday School. "By the time a child is five years old, the pattern is made. It may be possible to change the direction older children are going, but it's much easier to mold them early than it is to retrain them."

One of the department's main goals is to teach the children to pray. One lad who learned to talk to God in Sunday School was with his mother when she had to drive the family's old half-ton truck with its stick shift. Frankie, sensing his mother's apprehension, bowed his head and prayed aloud, "Dear Jesus, please help Mommy to drive this truck and keep us safe, Amen." Then he confidently said, "OK, Mommy, we can go now."

Mike is another example of the children's dependence on prayer. He was four years old when his two-year-old brother fell and cut his lip. It was bleeding profusely and his mother was gripped by sudden panic. "Oh, what are we going to do?" she said. Mike looked calmly up at her. "Let's pray about it, Mommy."

In every class the twos and threes are encouraged to pray for their own pains and for the illnesses of members of their family, no matter how simple they may seem.

"It may only be a skinned knee to us," one of the teachers says, "but it is a matter of great importance to the children. There are so many little hurts that we pray for them all at one time. If a mother or daddy is ill, they are prayed for as 'Susie's daddy,' or 'Tommy's mother.'"

One lad stopped the teacher in the middle of enumerating the prayer requests and asked for prayer for his mother. A couple of weeks later she was able to be in church again. "Look," the teacher said to him, "Jesus made your mommy better so she can be in church today." The child's face lit up with understanding.

"It is encouraging to all of us," a superintendent said, "to know that our kids are learning to depend on God for everyday problems. I'm convinced that boys and girls who learn to pray for their needs are going to think of turning to God with their needs as they grow older."

"We try to keep our entire Sunday School well equipped," Pastor Wollen says. "But we spend more money on our Twos and Threes department than on any other. We want quality enough to pay for it here. We keep everything in excellent condition."

With adequate space, the department is able to effectively use the Sunday School material available (Scripture Press materials are used in all Sunday School Departments above the nursery level). They installed the learning centers recommended by Sunday School authorities for holding the attention of kids in the younger ages, and to recruit staff to take care of them.

"One learning center might be on nature," Mrs. Stewart says. "In the spring the children will plant seeds and watch the growth from Sunday to Sunday. It gives us an opportunity to stress the fact that God takes care of us by providing plants for food to eat."

Another could be the housekeeping learning center. Here the kids would learn about Adam and Eve and Mary and Martha. Anything around the home that has to do with housekeeping is used for learning. The teacher is constantly making spiritual applications the children can understand and learn to follow.

Another learning center is God's house. The kids have a chance to build a church with blocks. "We are building God's house," the teacher would say. "We love God's house. We love to go to God's house, don't we?"

In an interesting way the child is exposed to God's love

and the proper attitude and conduct one should have in church.

There is also a book nook where different books are read to the kids every Sunday. As in most Sunday Schools, a considerable amount of eating goes on. It becomes a teaching occasion. Apples, honey and bread, or a teaspoonful of ice cream and a cone are favorites. The teacher reads a book about God giving these things, and the children learn to say, "Please" and "Thank you." The next Sunday they tell what they have learned about food.

When a child comes in on Sunday morning, the superintendent is always at the door to greet him. Then she escorts the child to the love-gift center. This is a table with a bank shaped like a church and a large mirror beside it.

While the youngster is putting his offering in the bank, she says, "I am giving my love gift because I love Jesus." She feels it is important for children to know that their money will help to buy books and Bibles and other items they use in their department. Then she has the child look into the mirror and ask him who he is looking at. He repeats his own name, and the superintendent continues: "Who does Tommy love?" "Jesus." Then she says, "Jesus loves you and He loves me too."

After the story the boys and girls visit the learning centers in turn. When a child stays in one center too long, the teacher moves him along with a suggestion.

About five or ten minutes after 10 o'clock, a brief "church service" is held to acquaint children with some of the forms of a worship service they will share with their parents at a later age. Then they return to their classes. The younger departments continue for three hours to allow parents to attend the morning service undisturbed.

The Sunday School seeks out husband and wife teams

for their younger departments. The requirements for both men and women teachers are the same, and they are approached in the same way.

"Love is the most important quality," Mrs. Stewart says, "and natural rapport with children is next. Two teachers can have the same love and can tell a story in almost the same way, but one will have the class enthralled and under control while the other may have discipline problems."

Her own daughter recognized this when she brought her guitar and sang for the kids. After the first class period she told her mother, "It's not going to work, Mom, that's not my bag."

In order to help the various superintendents have the right type of teachers, Pastor Wollen produced a handbook with the assistance of Rosie Roth who was director of Christian education at the time. Among other things, it asks:

"(As a teacher) am I putting in the hours in prayer, preparation, and follow-up that I know Christ would require of Himself in the same situation?" the handbook asks. "Do I possess in my own life the characteristics which I want to develop in my students?"

It also lists 10 points the late writer-publisher Henrietta C. Mears set down for herself when she first took a Sunday School class. It provides some of the answers to discipline problems and tells the teacher how to cope with them, and it goes into some of the basic needs for any class or department.

The results of the Sunday School are not limited to those who belong. The outreach goes far beyond the enrollment of the classes.

"We have several entire families worshipping with us who first got interested in the church through one member coming to Sunday school," Pastor Wollen says. "Now the father and mother and the other kids are following Christ. I feel the church owes a debt of gratitude to the faithful who work so hard in our Sunday School week after week."

The success of her department at Cedar Mill has brought Mrs. Stewart many invitations from other churches to take part in Sunday School workshops. At one church in Oregon a young man was particularly excited about Cedar Mill's care for children during the parents' church time. His own church thought the only way to make children like church was to get them into the regular worship services when they were very young.

"We had been on that route," Mrs. Stewart says. "I could sympathize with them, yet we learned there is a much better way of handling the situation."

The congregation at Cedar Mill agrees that their church has found a better way for both children and their parents —and growing families are the happy result.

9

A Family Affair

Raymond was born to a family in the congregation shortly after Al Wollen came to Cedar Mill Bible Church. At the age of six, Raymond was run over by a truck, suffering injuries that brought him near death for three days. For an entire year after his release from the hospital he was in a full body cast. Almost miraculously, he survived the accident without permanent physical effects, but the ordeal made profound changes in his personality.

"Not realizing how deeply he felt about any creature suffering pain," his father relates, "I took him deer hunting when he was in his early teens. The sight of the dead animal nauseated him."

In high school years Raymond was torn by a desire to please everyone: his classmates, his parents, and the people at church. It seemed almost inevitable that he would yield to the pressures of his friends and be carried into the things that ruled their lives. He slid into the drug scene and was deeply mired in it for five years. The climax came when authorities began to arrest the people he was associated with, and Ray was sure he would be next. In panic he returned home.

"By this time he was suffering from such severe mental disorders that we felt we had no choice but to commit him to a state institution," his father recalls. Instead, he asked to go with his folks on a two-week trip to an isolated area in the mountains. The retreat went so well they decided to keep Ray with them the rest of the summer. During these months Ray turned his life completely over to Christ and began to get on track again.

"I chanced to overhear Ray talking with a friend on the phone not long after he came back to Christ," his father confides. "He said, 'Nobody in this church ever criticized me or found fault with me. All they did was to pray for me.' "

That statement seems to characterize the Cedar Mill Bible Church family. Their love for each other and for those outside God's family welds them into a warm fellowship.

"When I first came to church here," a college-age girl says, "I was so lonely and discouraged I didn't think I could continue to stay in school. I didn't know anything about this church, but as I sat down I prayed silently, asking God to send someone to touch me—to love me.

"A couple of minutes later a middle-aged lady leaned over and took me by the arm. She asked my name and wanted to know if I was a visitor. Then she said she was so happy to have me here. After the service she came and talked with me again, introducing me to several others. I've never felt lonely here since."

Mrs. Leona Fey, one of the charter members of the congregation, tells of a Jewish girl who also experienced the love of the people in the church. After she received Christ as her Saviour, her dismayed parents had her charged with insanity. A hearing was held to determine whether she should be forcibly confined in an institution.

"Most of the congregation turned out for the trial," Mrs. Fey recalls. "Men missed work to be there, showing their concern. I think that indicates the spirit and unity we see here."

This concern for each other shows itself in many ways. A few years ago one of the men in the congregation came to the pastor with a pleasant problem. Gardening was his hobby and he was raising far more vegetables than he could possibly use. He wondered if there was something that could be done to get his excess food into the hands of those who would like to have it. Pastor Wollen, also an avid gardener, found himself in the same predicament.

"It isn't right to let food go to waste when there are people who would like to have it," he told his wife. He thought there must be church members who lacked the time, the space, or the inclination to tend a garden.

With the help of the church custodian he placed a long table in the foyer, and every Sunday morning the pastor and his gardener-parishioners brought vegetables of all kinds for those who wanted to take them.

At first people were reluctant. "I didn't bring anything to put out," one woman objected when the pastor asked if she wanted some of the fresh produce. She had the idea it was an exchange. Further explanation and encouragement from the pulpit cleared up the confusion, and eventually three ten-foot tables were channeling the abundance to the congregation.

Many churches have a deacon board charged with the spiritual welfare of the congregation and the responsibility of visiting the sick and the elderly. At Cedar Mill the deacons have also worked out program activities for them, including regular outings and a successful foster-grandparents program.

"Our first effort at outside activities for the elderly didn't work out well," admits Bryan Owens, chairman of the deacons. "We arranged for a trip to the beach, including a meal at a nice restaurant. On paper the idea was great. But we failed to consider the debilitating effect of infirmities on the aged. Only 12 of the 120 or so who were eligible made the trip, and most of them stayed in the car.

"We learned that in working with the elderly," adds Owens, "we had to keep the physical condition of the people constantly in mind. This meant having a simple affair that did not last too long or require any semi-strenuous activity. Consequently it is easy to develop something for senior citizens. They are the most appreciative group in any church."

The foster-grandparents program is so loosely organized that some might not call it a program at all. Owens' experiences are typical.

"Our family visits two couples regularly," he relates. "We had a casual acquaintance with them when we first stopped by to see them, but that soon changed. We found them becoming like 'family' to us. We looked forward to the visits and enjoyed having them over for meals.

"Our kids have come to appreciate them. It's been a blessing to my wife and me to see how the kids pray for our elderly friends and are concerned about them. This is particularly true of our 14-year-old daughter. Her own grandparents aren't nearby, and she has adopted our older friends as her grandparents. I sometimes think she would rather go and see them than be with kids her own age.

"We simply encourage people in the congregation to visit

the elderly and do simple things for them," Owens explains. "I guess a part of our church concept is that everyone who attends is part of our church family, and we should be concerned about their physical, mental, and spiritual welfare. Last Easter we had almost 100 Easter lilies decorating the church, and after the morning service the pastor suggested that some might take lilies to some of the elderly and shut-ins. Many shared this beauty with their Christian friends."

Pastor Wollen visited an elderly widow soon after the funeral of her husband and learned that her memory was so faulty she could not be trusted to take care of herself. The refrigerator contained plenty of food, but she didn't know whether she had anything to eat in the house, and she could not recall whether she had taken her medicine for high blood pressure.

Roberta and Al Wollen took care of her the next day, Saturday, then on Sunday he asked people to volunteer to see that Grandma Griffen's house was cleaned, that she had at least one well-balanced meal a day, and that she took her medicine properly.

"There was no problem in getting people to help her," Wollen says. "For a period of three months women of the church took turns going over to the widow's house to take care of her. We would have continued, but her health deteriorated to the point where it seemed advisable that she have continual personal care."

A man in the church was in a similar situation. The church found a nursing home for him, and he is visited regularly by members of the congregation.

One of the nurses told an elder of the church who stopped by to see this man, "He is one of the most cheerful men we have in the home. It may be because he has more visitors and people who love him than anybody else in the entire home." She paused a moment. "How does it happen that he has so many friends?"

"Well," the visitor replied, "he just belongs to our church family. We all minister to him."

"The nursing home and the nursing ministry would be wonderful if all the people were loved and cared for as this man is," commented the nurse.

And so would all churches be wonderful in the expression of such love and care. With the God of love as our Father, even this is possible in His family.

10

Serving the Whole Person

Cedar Mill Bible, like other evangelical congregations, is primarily concerned with the spiritual condition of the people it is striving to reach, but the members are also aware of the importance of meeting the physical needs of their own people and others in touch with the church.

"We have a sizable deacons' fund," Pastor Wollen explains, "to help people who are hurting financially. The deacons spend this money as they see fit without asking permission of anyone or making an accounting. This is to assure absolute secrecy."

Meeting physical needs is regarded as a means of showing the compassion of Christ for the whole person.

"Probably the only difference between our deacons' fund and that of most churches is the size of it," Wollen continues. "It is so important that recently one member of our congregation made a $1,500 contribution to it. It has been used, for example, to buy food for those who have no money, to help an unemployed man to save his house, and a mother to pay her rent and buy clothing for herself and her children."

Portland was hard hit by the recession of 1974-75. One young man who was laid off was in danger of losing his home. The deacons' fund came to the rescue, picking up his payments and helping in other ways until the economy improved and he went back to work again.

"We never ask anyone we help to repay what we have given him," Pastor Wollen says, "but that frequently happens. I suppose we gave the young man who was about to lose his house something like $4,000 before he was called back to work. Even though we hadn't asked him to repay us, the first Sunday in January 1976 he made the first payment to the deacons' fund. He says he is going to repay all that the church invested in him."

Another young man started a business without adequate training and soon found himself in difficulty. He was unfamiliar with factors that figured in realistic pricing, and was negligent in filing withholding and Social Security payments to the government for his employees. As a result he found himself in need of a sizable amount of money immediately. He went to the bank but his credit rating would not permit them to make him a loan.

The deacons' fund came to his rescue, providing the money he needed to keep the IRS from closing his doors, but that was only the first chapter of the story. The deacons made arrangements for an accountant and a retired businessman (both members of Cedar Mill Bible Church) to take over his books and to help him in pricing and in establishing profitable business procedures. In addition, a number of women volunteered to work in his little store without pay so he could be spared the necessity of having to put out money for wages during that critical period. In the next six or eight months the accountant and the retired businessman taught the young man the things he should have known before venturing into business on his own.

A young mother who moved to Portland found the deacons' fund the answer to a difficult situation. She came to Portland with her three children after the death of her husband. When her plight first came to Wollen's attention, she was living with her family in a dilapidated apartment. She had no furniture except a rickety card table and a couple of apple boxes for chairs. There were two sleeping bags for the children, but she only had a tattered quilt for herself.

On Sunday morning the pastor told enough of her story to stir concern. "When you register your attendance this morning," he said, "turn the card over and write down what you have that you can spare for this young woman. She needs everything."

Monday morning after the secretary checked the attendance cards, she had a list three pages long of items that members of the congregation were willing to share. Wollen took the list to the woman and asked her to mark the items she wanted.

Women from the church came to the widow's apartment and scrubbed the walls and floors left filthy by previous tenants. They cleaned and papered and painted until it was bright and cheery. Their husbands hauled the furniture in and arranged it the way the astonished mother wanted it, put up a television antenna and hooked up the washer and dryer. The dilapidated apartment became a suitable home for the woman and her children.

The woman had a job but there was still the problem of paying a baby-sitter until she got on her feet enough to carry that burden herself. Again the women in the church stepped into the gap. They took turns caring for the three children for several months without charge.

"It wasn't long," Pastor Wollen recounted, "until that young mother received Christ as her Saviour."

The church's concern for people has brought some unusual opportunities to share Christ with those who do not know Him. As Wollen was leaving the church one evening after a board meeting, he saw a young woman in the parking lot. Something prompted him to speak as she was turning away from him. "My, what a pretty dress," he exclaimed.

She thanked him and then asked hesitantly, "Is there a minister here now?"

He told her he was the pastor, and she said she would like to talk with him. As they went into the building to his study, Wollen saw that the attractive dress was actually a wedding dress. Her story was a familiar tale of marriage, misunderstandings, and the heartbreak of divorce. She and her husband had continued to see each other after their divorce and she had hopes that they would one day be reconciled. That morning all her hopes had been shattered. He had phoned her with the startling announcement: "Our divorce is final today—and I am engaged to someone else. So I don't want you to call me or write anymore."

She had stumbled through her job that day as though in a fog. At home she had put on her wedding dress and gone out with the intention of killing herself. As she passed the church, she felt drawn to stop just when Pastor Wollen came out to go home.

"She was in abject despair when I started to talk with her," he relates, "but after a little while I helped her to see that the Lord is a personal Saviour. I said God had directed her to the church because He loved her and was watching over her. I told her, 'That man had to kick a big hole in your heart so the Lord Jesus Christ could come in and heal it, giving you a new life.' "

She invited Christ into her heart that evening and went home with real peace and joy, turning what could have been a tragedy into victory and newness. The next morning Wollen phoned a couple of young women of the church and alerted them to the situation. They promised to take her under their wings and help to fill the emptiness in her life. Their first act was to invite her to a weekend retreat that began the following afternoon.

The concern of the church family for physical needs is also reflected in its prayer chain, a program of prayer partners, and in the prayer at the Sunday morning worship services.

The prayer chain, consisting of approximately 50 people, is set up so an individual with an immediate need for prayer can phone anyone in the chain and everyone else will be notified.

"We've seen many dramatic answers to prayer," a member of the congregation said, "but there has been a side benefit I didn't think about until I was deeply involved. That is the bond of fellowship and love that prayer fosters. It is so comforting to know that people care enough about you to pray when you have a special problem."

The program of prayer partners has a simple format. It started with one of the women's home Bible classes and spread. The plan is for two people to agree to get in touch with each other in person or by phone at least once a week to pray for each other.

"There are certain types of problems an individual might hesitate to take to a prayer chain of 50 people," Pastor Stewart says, "but he would bring that matter to the attention of one good friend who could be trusted to keep it secret."

"When my prayer partner and I phone each other," one man revealed, "we don't ask about the weather or how things are going; one of us will pray, and then the other prays, and we hang up. If we have anything else to talk about, we phone again so we always carry out the main purpose of the weekly calls."

Every Sunday morning people bring their special requests at each service. Six members of the council go to the front, read written requests of the morning, and together with the pastor, pray specifically for them. These requests are unsigned.

"Sometimes there is a request that requires more personal attention than prayer," one of the board members says. "It might be a prayer for food or a specific material need with which the deacons could help. We ask the person who made the request to identify himself to the pastor so the church can be of more service in that area. Most of the requests, however, are for spiritual or physical needs that require no action on the part of the deacons."

Cedar Mill Bible believes Philippians 4:19 is true—"My God shall supply all your need according to His riches in glory by Christ Jesus." And He uses the Cedar Mill people as loving channels.

11

Living Word and Works

What makes Cedar Mill Bible Church so unusual? Some say it is the development of home Bible studies. Some say it is the effective preaching and leadership of the pastor. Some point to the council-unanimous agreement system of government. Others might point to the innovative, dedicated children's ministry.

Actually, it is all of these things and more. The secret perhaps can be expressed in a single word: love.

At Cedar Mill there is demonstrated love for the individual, both within the church family and outside. That love is shown within the home Bible studies where believers are strengthened and unbelievers are encouraged. It is evidenced in the life-related teaching of Pastor Wollen and the person-conscious ministry of his assistant, Walter Stewart. It shows in the hospitality and sacrifice of the pastors' wives, Roberta and Laura. It shines in the consideration given a dissenting voter in the church council, and in the teamwork with poor athletes in sports competition.

"Attending church here is an experience in love," one Christian said after his first visit. Further examination of church life confirms that appraisal. Love is felt because the members know that God is love and that they are to be like their God. Accordingly, this principle is becoming a day-by-day reality.

"For as we have many members in one body, and all members have not the same office: So we, being many, are one body in Christ, and every one members one of another. Having then gifts differing according to the grace that is given to us, whether prophecy, let us prophesy according to the proportion of faith; or ministry, let us wait on our ministering: or he that teacheth, on teaching; Or he that exhorteth, on exhortation: he that giveth, let him do it with simplicity; he that ruleth, with diligence; he that sheweth mercy, with cheerfulness. Let love be without dissimulation. Abhor that which is evil; cleave to that which is good. Be kindly affectioned one to another with brotherly love; in honour preferring one another; not slothful in business; fervent in spirit; serving the Lord; rejoicing in hope; patient in tribulation; continuing instant in prayer; distributing to the necessity of saints; given to hospitality. Bless them which persecute you: bless, and curse not. Rejoice with them that do rejoice, and weep with them that weep. Be of the same mind one toward another. Mind not high things, but condescend to men of low estate. Be not wise in your own conceits. Recompense to no man evil for evil. Provide things honest in the sight of all men. If it be possible, as much as lieth in you, live peaceably with all men. Dearly beloved, avenge not yourselves, but rather give place unto wrath: for it is written, Vengeance is mine; I will repay, saith the Lord. Therefore if thine enemy hunger, feed him; if he thirst, give him drink: for in so doing thou shalt heap coals of fire on his head. Be not overcome of evil, but overcome evil with good" (Rom. 12:4-21).